SILHOUETTES
IN CROSS STITCH

SILHOUETTES
IN CROSS STITCH

JULIE HASLER

DAVID PORTEOUS

CHUDLEIGH · DEVON

Four Burners,
Thanks for the pleasure
you give through your music—Slater,
Julie.

A CIP catalogue record for this book
is available from the British Library

ISBN 1 870586 11 5

Published by David Porteous
PO Box 5
Chudleigh
Newton Abbot
Devon
TQ13 0YZ

© 1993 Julie Hasler

Designed by Vic Giolitto
Typeset by Colin Bakké Typesetting, Exeter
Printed in Great Britain by
BPCC Paulton Books Limited

CONTENTS

INTRODUCTION

There is evidence that a type of silhouette existed in the Middle Ages, but the form failed to become popular, largely because of superstition. Silhouettes were associated with bad luck by peoples of many faiths, and, just as some people today regard photographs with alarm as in some way being able to appropriate their souls, so the shadow representation of a person's appearance was felt in some way to be tampering with fate and inviting disaster.

The silhouette, often referred to as "shadow" or "profile" art in portraiture, can be created in various ways. Traditionally, the subject was seated between a strong light and a waxed or oiled screen, and the artist blackened or painted the area of shadow cast by the light on the screen. The distance of the sitter from the screen could be varied to increase or decrease the size of the shadow cast. A more sophisticated version used a type of projector to vary the size of shadow.

As paper and scissors became more widely available, another form of silhouette became widely practised. The artist would cut out a portrait from a piece of black paper, and accomplished painters who turned their hands to this technique produced some extremely fine work. This method became popular in western Europe in the 18th century.

The word silhouette did not become current

in Britain until the mid-18th century. It derives from the French finance minister Etienne de Silhouette (1709–67), who planned to introduce some drastic financial economies that would have severely restricted the expenditure of the royal household. Within months, Silhouette was forced to resign, an object of ridicule throughout the country. His hobby was profile cutting, and his unpopularity led to this cheap form of portraiture becoming contemptuously associated with his name.

During the 18th and early 19th centuries a wide range of styles and materials became popular in Europe, and the increasing vogue for silhouettes is believed to have been in part a reaction against the elaborately decorated and ornamented architecture and interiors of the time. The profile artists worked in a variety of media, including paper, ivory, wax, card, glass and plaster, often introducing a colour in addition to the simple black and white. Crimson on black was especially popular, and was supposedly based on the decorative style of Greek pottery.

Among the notable artists who worked in the medium was the Danish author of fairy tales, Hans Christian Andersen (1805–75), who was a skilled cutter who generally favoured white paper. John André (1751–80), a British soldier who served with the British army in America and who was captured by the Americans and hanged as a spy, is remembered for his fine series of cut portraits in black paper. Johann Friedrich (1753–1823) was a French portraitist who worked in Germany and England, while probably the best known and finest French paper cutter was Augustin Edouart (1789–1861). John Field (b. 1771) was a profilist to Princess Caroline of Brunswick (wife of George IV) and the Princess Augusta.

In 1839 Louis Jacques Mandé Daguerre, the French painter and pioneer of photography, published details of the process he had developed of using sunlight to obtain permanent pictures on a chemically treated glass or metal plate. The introduction of daguerreotypes put an end to the wide-spread demand for portraits created by the silhouette method, and the silhouette artist was ousted from his previously eminent position. Fewer and fewer people took up the art of the cutting and painting profiles, and the art form began to fall from favour.

Although the art of cutting out paper profiles may have died out, cross stitch lends itself perfectly to the tradition of producing outlines in a single colour on a background of a contrasting colour. Black on white always looks extremely effective and sophisticated, but fabrics and stranded cottons are now available in such a wealth of colours that even the same outline worked in different colourways can be made to look subtly different and personal.

In this book I have included some charts for what might be regarded as "traditional" silhouettes – that is, profile portraits. If you are artistic you can, of course, make your own portraits of your friends or relatives, but even if you are not especially artistic, you can, by using photographs and photocopiers, prepare your own charts quite easily. I have also included a variety of designs to indicate how wide a range of patterns can be worked in just two colours. Symmetrical, geometric designs have always been popular, and they can be especially effective when they are worked in two contrasting colours to make cushion covers, place mats, curtain ties and runners, for example. Two colours can also be used, however, to make pictures of people and animals and to illustrate stories, nursery rhymes and poetry. The designs in this book include a wide range of motifs and illustrations, which can be used singly or combined with each other, to create some unusual and highly attractive projects.

MATERIALS
AND TECHNIQUES

MATERIALS

To complete the projects you will need the following.

♦ A small, blunt tapestry needle. A number 24 or a number 26 will be suitable for all the projects in this book.
♦ Evenweave fabric. Use a fabric on which you can easily count the threads, both vertically and horizontally. Evenweave fabrics, such as Aida, Hardanger and Ainring, are available in a wide selection of colours — ecru, red, blue, green, yellow, for example, as well as black and white — and in a variety of thread counts. Do not use a plainweave fabric; not only is it extremely difficult to keep the stitches evenly sized, but the design will become distorted.
♦ DMC cotton. All the projects in this book were worked in DMC stranded cotton, the number of strands that are used depending on the fabric used. The colours and the number of threads used are indicated for each project.
♦ Embroidery hoop. A circular plastic or wooden embroidery hoop, 10, 12.5 or 15cm (4, 5 or 6in) in diameter and with a screw-type tension adjuster, is ideal for cross stitch.
♦ A pair of embroidery scissors. You will need a pair of sharp, pointed scissors, which you should keep especially for sewing.

PREPARING TO WORK

To prevent the edges of the fabric from unravelling you can either protect them by folding over lengths of masking-tape along each edge or you can whip stitch each edge by hand or stay stitch the edges on a machine.

Where you make your first stitch is important because it will dictate the position of the finished design on your fabric. Find the exact centre of the chart — draw a pencil down and across from the arrows on the chart, and where the lines intersect is the centre of that chart. Find the centre of your fabric by folding it in half, first vertically and then horizontally, pinching it along the folds so that the crease can be faintly seen; again, where the creases intersect is the centre of the fabric. You may wish to mark these lines with basting stitches.

You should begin your cross stitch at the top of the design. Count the squares up from the centre point and then out to the left or right as far as the first symbol. Remember that each square on the chart represents a square on your fabric, and each symbol represents a different colour.

If you are using an embroidery hoop, place the portion of the fabric on which you are going to be working over the inner hoop and gently push the outer ring over it. Carefully and evenly pull the fabric until it is as taut as a drum in the hoop and the mesh is perfectly straight, tightening the screw as you do so. If you are right handed you will find it easier to work if the screw is in the "10 o'clock" position; if you are left handed, it should be at "1 o'clock". This will help prevent the thread from catching in the screw as you sew. While you are working you will find that you will need to tighten the screw from time to time to keep the material taut. It is easier to stitch when the fabric is under tension because you can more easily push your needle through the holes without piercing the fibres of the fabric.

When you stitch with stranded cotton, always cut off a suitable length to work with and separate the appropriate number of strands. For example, if the design calls for two strands of cotton, use two separate strands, not one strand doubled.

TECHNIQUES
Cross Stitch

To make your first stitch, bring your needle up from the wrong side of your work through a hole in the fabric (Fig. 1) at the left-hand end of a row of stitches of the same colour. Fasten the thread by holding a short length of thread on the underside of the fabric and securing it with the first two or three stitches you make (Fig. 2). Never use knots to fasten the end of your thread; they will make it impossible for the finished work to lie absolutely flat and small bumps will be visible from the front.

Next, bring your needle across one square to the right and one square above on a left-to-right diagonal and insert it in the hole (Fig. 1). Half of the stitch is now made. Continue in this way, working across the row until you have completed the appropriate number of stitches.

Your stitches should lie diagonally on the top of your work and vertically on the wrong side. Then complete the top half of your stitch by crossing back from right to left to make the "×" (Fig. 3). Work back along the row to complete all the crosses (Fig. 4). Vertical rows of stitches can be worked as shown in Fig. 5.

Cross stitch can also be worked by completing each cross as you come to it, as you would work an isolated stitch. This method works just as well. It is simply a matter of personal preference. The only point you must remember is that all the top stitches must lie in the same direction.

Finish off each length of thread by running your needle under four or more stitches on the wrong side (Fig. 6) and by cutting off the end close to your work.

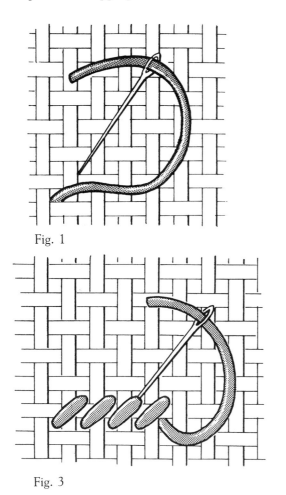

Fig. 1

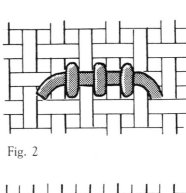

Fig. 2

Fig. 3

Fig. 4

Fig. 5

Backstitch

In some of the designs backstitch is used for outlines or for some of the finer details. Work any backstitch when you have finished all the cross stitch.

Always use one strand fewer than you did for the cross stitch. For example, if the cross stitch was worked with three strands, you would use two strands of cotton for the backstitch. If only one strand of cotton was used for the cross stitch, you would also use one strand for the backstitch.

Backstitch is worked from hole to hole, and you can work horizontally, vertically or diagonally (Fig. 7). Take care that you do not pull the stitches too tightly or the contrast of colour will be lost. Finish off the thread as you would for cross stitch.

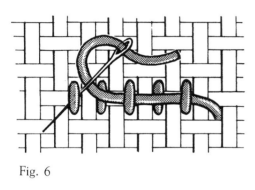

Fig. 6

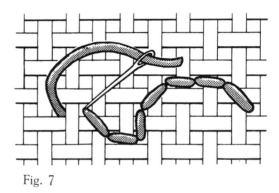

Fig. 7

♦ When you are stitching take care that you do not pull the fabric out of shape. You can do this by making all your stitches in two distinct movements — straight up through a hole in fabric and then straight down — and by keeping your fabric taut on a hoop while you work. Do not pull the thread too tight; it should be snug, not tight. If you use this method you will find that the thread lies just where you want it to and will not pull the material out of shape.

♦ If your thread becomes twisted while you work, drop your needle and allow it to untwist itself. Do not continue to work with a twisted thread because it will look thinner and not cover the material well.

♦ Never leave your needle in the area of the design when it is not in use. No matter how good the needle may be, it could rust in time and mark your work permanently.

♦ Do not carry threads across open expanses of fabric. If you are working separate areas of the same colour, finish off and begin again. Loose threads, especially of dark colours, will be visible from the right side of the work when the project is completed.

♦ When you have completed the design, iron your work by placing it, right side down, on a soft towel and pressing it under a slightly damp cotton cloth.

LOOKING AFTER YOUR WORK

You may at some stage find that your projects need to be laundered. This is not a problem if you simply follow the advice given by DMC with its six-stranded cotton. You should always wash your embroidery separately.

COTTON OR LINEN FABRIC	SYNTHETIC FABRIC
Recommended washing	
Wash in warm, soapy water. Rinse thoroughly. Squeeze without twisting and hang to dry. Iron on reverse side under two layers of white linen.	Not recommended.
Bleaching or whitening agent	
Dilute according to the manufacturer's instructions. Pre-soak the embroidery in clear water, then soak for 5 minutes in a solution of about 20ml (1 tbsp) of disinfectant in about 1 litre (2 pints) of cold water. Rinse thoroughly in cold water.	These instructions are recommended if the white of the fabric is not of a high standard. If the fabric is pure white (that is, white with a bluish tinge) do not use a bleaching or whitening agent.
Dry cleaning	
Avoid dry cleaning. Some spot removers (benzene and trichloroethylene) can be used for small, occasional stains.	Not recommended, even for small, occasional stains.

SUPPLIERS

Brass frames, greetings cards, bell pulls, brass and wooden trays and so on are available from:

Framecraft Miniatures Ltd
148–150 High Street
Aston
Birmingham B6 4US
UK

Ireland Needlecraft Pty Ltd
2–4 Keppel Drive
Hallam
Victoria 3803
Australia

The Embroidery Shop
Greville-Parker
286 Queen Street
Masterton
New Zealand

Anne Brinkley Designs Inc
761 Palmer Avenue
Holmdel
NJ 97733
USA

Gay Bowles Sales Inc
PO Box 1060
Janesville
WI 53547
USA

Stranded embroidery cottons and evenweave fabrics are available from:

DMC Creative World Ltd
Pullman Road
Wigston
Leicester LE8 2DY
UK

The DMC Corporation
Port Kearney Bld.
#10 South Kearney
NJ 07032-0650
USA

DMC Needlecraft Pty
PO Box 317
Earlswood 2206
New South Wales 2204
Australia

Graph paper is available from:

H.W. Peel & Company Ltd
Norwester House
Fairway Drive
Greenford
Middlesex UB6 8PW
UK

Zweigart evenweave fabrics are available from:

Joan Toggitt Ltd
Zweigart Sales Office
Weston Canal Plaza
2 Riverview Drive
Somerset
NJ 08873
USA

Foot stools, tapestry frames, fire screens, sewing frames, sewing stools and so on are available from:

The Woodhouse
111 High Street
Rye
East Sussex
TN31 7TS
UK

ACKNOWLEDGEMENTS

I should like to thank the following people for their invaluable help in the skilful sewing up of the embroideries in this book: Odette Harrison, Maureen Hipgrave, Barbara Hodgkinson, Allison Mortley, Joyce Formby, Jenny Whitlock, Jennie Gardener, Elizabeth Aldridge, Linda Potter, Dawn Parmley, Karen Lipscombe and Libby Shaw.

I should also like to thank the following companies, which have contributed embroidery threads, fabrics, accessories and graph paper for use in this book: Framecraft Miniatures Ltd, DMC Creative World Ltd and H.W. Peel & Company Ltd.

SEWING BOX

THIS ITEM is part of a beautiful range of self-upholster decorative furniture that is available from craft suppliers and department stores. The sewing box is designed to take a needlework design measuring 30 × 38cm (12 × 15in).

YOU WILL NEED

1 piece of white 18-count Ainring, 45 × 53cm (17¾ × 20¾in)
No. 26 tapestry needle
DMC six-strand embroidery cotton
Calico or similar fabric, the same size as the Ainring
Self-cover sewing box
Tape measure
5mm (¼in) tacks
Hammer

1. Complete the embroidery, using two strands for the cross stitch and one strand for the backstitch.
2. The gap between the top of the sewing box and the frame is designed to accept a piece of embroidered tapestry (needlepoint). Because you are using a thinner material, you should cover the top with a material such as calico so that your finished embroidery fits snugly into the frame. Follow the directions given below for both the calico lining and the embroidery.
3. Remove the top of the sewing box by undoing the screws which are recessed into the underframe. Keep them aside for later.
4. Lay the sewing box top on a flat surface with the pad uppermost. Measure the distance from one edge to the other, making sure that you take the full distance into account. Do this from side to side and from back to front. Add 7.5cm (3in) to both measurements so that you know how much material you will need.
5. Turn over 5mm (¼in) of raw edge all around and tack down. Lay the material, right side down, on a flat surface. Place the sewing box top, pad down, in the centre of the material so that an equal amount shows all around the top.

Squeeze the pad down on to the material along one of the long edges; you may find that kneeling on it helps. Bring the material over the edge and tack it down with 5mm (¼in) tacks, hammering the tacks through the stitched double layer. Work outwards, bringing the material over the edge as you insert tacks. Keep the material edge straight and an even distance from the edge of the top. Insert a tack about

every 4cm (1½in). Work to both corners.

6. Squeeze the sewing box top down along the opposite edge and insert tacks as before.

7. Repeat the process along one of the short edges. This time, fold the material at the corners, pulling the folds inwards so that the material does not bulge outwards from the pad. Repeat the process on the last edge.

8. If you wish, sew or glue a piece of calico or similar material to the underside of the pad before you replace it on the sewing box to give a neat finish.

9. Replace the top on the sewing box, gently pressing it in to the corners where the fit will be the tightest. Rescrew the top to the frame.

Note: The material can also be fixed using a staple gun or by lacing with fine twine or strong thread.

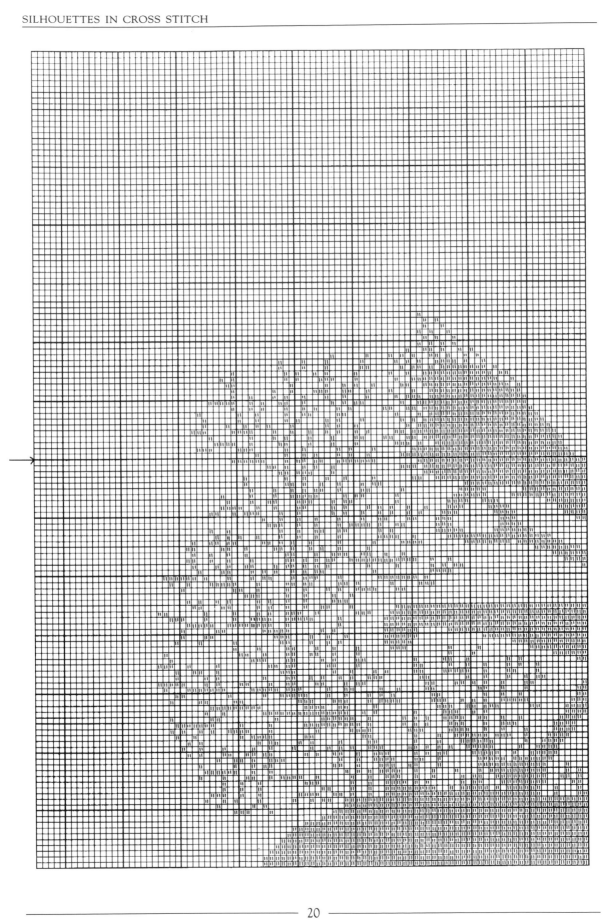

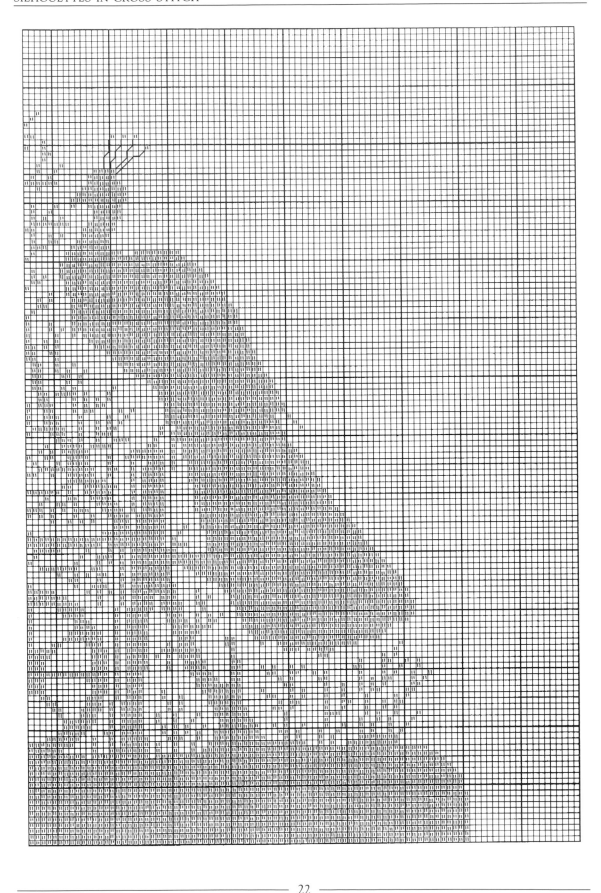

FRAMED MINIATURES

FRAMED MINIATURES

T HESE DELIGHTFUL miniature pictures will make an attractive addition to your home, whether you display them singly or in a group. Any of the designs would make a lovely gift. The materials quoted here are sufficient for one framed picture, 15cm (6in) in diameter.

YOU WILL NEED

1 round brass frame, 15cm (6in) in diameter
1 piece of cream, 28-count Quaker Cloth, 20.5 × 20.5cm (8 × 8in)
DMC six-strand embroidery cotton
No. 26 tapestry needle

1. Use one strand of embroidery cotton throughout to work your design. When it is complete, press if required.
2. Carefully dismantle all parts of the frame, and use the template provided to draw around your design, making sure that it is central. Very carefully cut out your embroidery along that line. If you think the material will fray, stitch a line of stay stitches around the edge or oversew the raw edge; alternatively use one of the proprietary "fray check" preparations.
3. Clean the glass and place it in the frame. Put your embroidery in position, then the thin card and finally the backing. Your frame is now complete.

COLLECTOR'S CABINET

COLLECTOR'S CABINET

ANOTHER UNUSUAL way
of displaying cross stitch
embroidery is in this
lovely collector's cabinet (see Suppliers,
page 17).

YOU WILL NEED
1 piece of 25-count Lugana, 15.5 × 15.5cm
 (6 × 6in)
DMC six-strand embroidery cotton
No. 26 tapestry needle
1 piece of batting, 15.5 × 15.5cm (6 × 6in)
Small collector's cabinet
Masking tape or fabric glue
Double-sided adhesive tape

1. Complete the embroidery, using one strand of
 the embroidery cotton throughout. Press the
 finished work if necessary.

2. Cover the grey mounting board provided with
 the collector's cabinet with batting, securing it
 with masking tape or fabric adhesive. Place the
 embroidery face down on a clean, flat surface
 and lay the mounting board centrally on it. Fold
 the corners of the fabric over the board, mitring
 them to give a neat appearance. Fold the
 remaining edges of the fabric over the board and
 secure them with masking tape.

3. Place the mounted embroidery in the cabinet
 recess, fixing it with adhesive or double-sided
 tape.

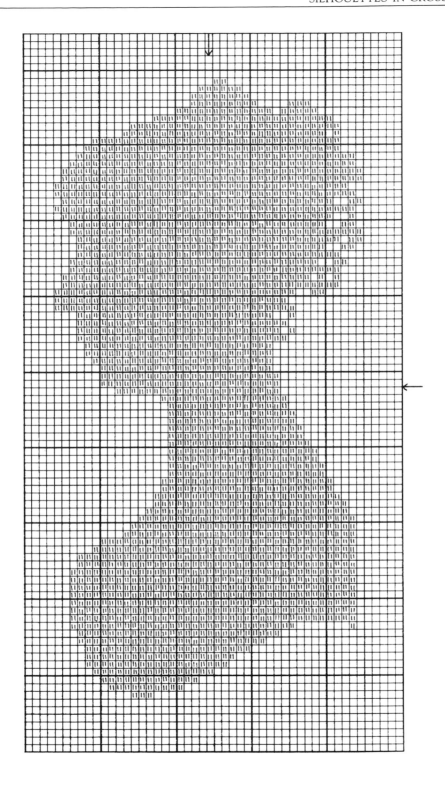

TABLE RUNNER

T HIS UNUSUAL Victorian-style
table runner would make an
eye-catching addition to any
room.

YOU WILL NEED

1 piece of white 18-count Ainring, 28 × 68.5cm
    (11 × 27in); this includes a 12mm (½in)
    seam allowance
2m (6ft 8in) lace, 2.5cm (1in) deep
DMC six-strand embroidery cotton
No. 26 tapestry needle
Sewing thread

1. Work the design from the charts using two
   strands of cotton and leaving 4cm (1½in) of
   clear fabric below the design and 27 clear fabric
   threads between each figure.
2. Pin and tack a 1cm (½in) hem all around the
   edge of the fabric.
3. Gather the lace evenly and pin it to the edges
   of the fabric on the wrong side of the work.
4. Machine or handstitch the lace into position.
   Remove the pins.

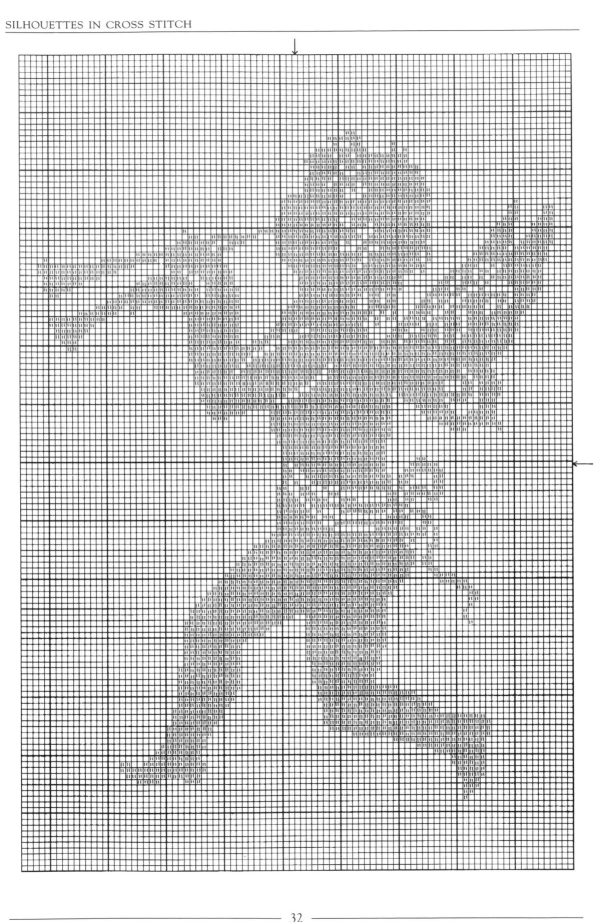

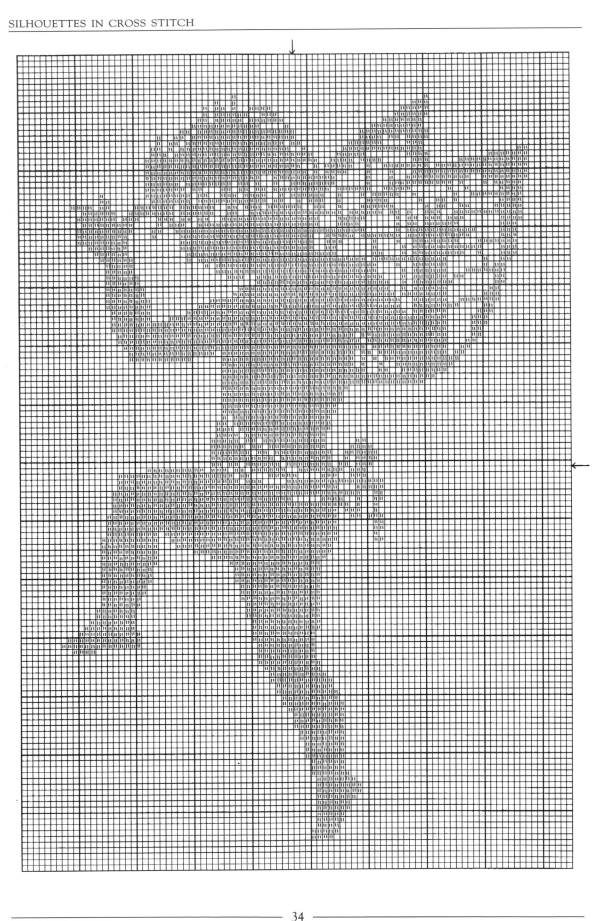

DRESSING-TABLE SET

THIS TRADITIONAL silver-plated dressing-table set, which is available from Framecraft Miniatures Ltd, makes a delightful accessory to any dressing-table. See Suppliers, page 17, for details.

YOU WILL NEED

Hand mirror with back, measuring 13 × 11.5cm (5 × 4½in)

Hair brush with back, measuring 10 × 9cm (4 × 3½in)

2 pieces of white 22-count Hardanger, 22 × 22cm (8½ × 8½in)

DMC six-strand embroidery cotton

No. 26 tapestry needle

1. Complete the cross stitch embroidery, using one strand of stranded cotton throughout. Press the completed work if necessary.
2. Place the finished embroidery face up on a firm, flat surface. Carefully disassemble all parts from the hand mirror and hair brush. Use the piece of acetate provided as your fabric cutting guide, positioning it over your embroidery until you

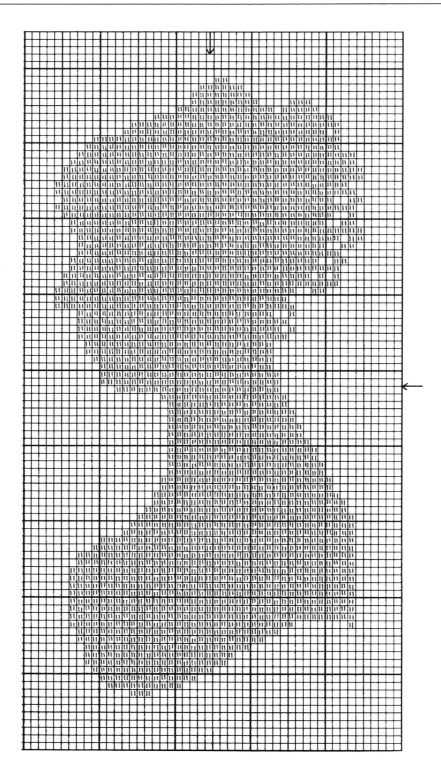

are happy with the effect. Hold the acetate down firmly with one hand and draw around it with a soft pencil. Cut your fabric to size. Oversew by hand or stay stitch around the raw edges if you wish, or apply a proprietary "fray check".

4. Assemble the hand mirror and hair brush according to the manufacturer's instructions.

FRAMED PICTURE

THIS PICTURE is based on the well-known folk tale about the Musicians of Bremen. We have chosen to work it in black on white, which makes a dramatic and eye-catching composition. However, it would look equally attractive in almost any other combination of colours. What better way is there to display your handiwork for all to admire than to give it a prominent position on the wall of your favourite room. The materials quoted will make one picture 50 × 32cm (20 × 12½in)

YOU WILL NEED
1 piece of 18-count white Ainring, 53 × 34cm (21 × 13½in)
DMC six-strand embroidery cotton
No. 26 tapestry needle
Mounting board 48 × 29cm (19 × 11½in)
Masking tape
Picture frame of your choice

1. Complete the cross stitch embroidery, placing it centrally on the Ainring and using two strands of stranded cotton for the cross stitch and one strand for the backstitch.
2. When you have completed the embroidery, press it so that it is perfectly flat and the threads of the Ainring are straight and ready for mounting.
3. Mount the embroidery by stretching it over the mounting board. Place the embroidery face down on a clean, flat surface and place the mounting board centrally over it. Fold one edge of the fabric over the mounting board (making sure that it is perfectly straight) and secure it with pins along the edge of the board. Secure the opposite edge in the same way, checking that the fabric is straight and taut on the board. Use masking tape to hold the fabric in place on the back of the mounting board and remove the pins.
4. Repeat this procedure on the remaining two edges. Your embroidery picture is now ready to be framed.
5. Insert the glass and mounted embroidery into your picture frame, add the backing board provided and secure it with rustproof tacks.

Cover the tacks with broad masking tape to neaten and prevent dust from entering the frame. If you wish, you could take it to a professional framer.

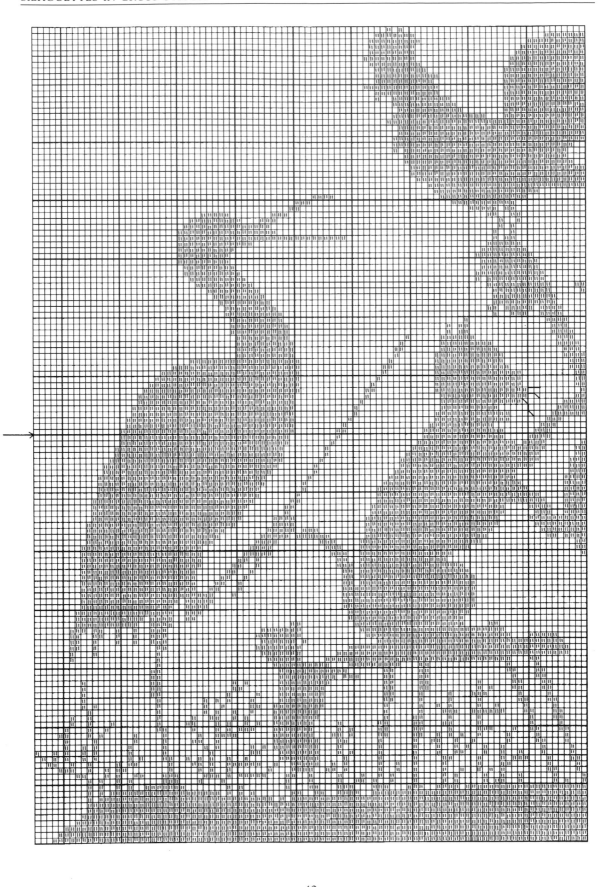

TEA TRAY

TEA TRAY

WHEN FRIENDS call in for tea, impress them with this beautiful tray, lovingly embroidered and mounted under glass. The materials quoted here are sufficient to make one tray measuring 24 × 24cm (9½ × 9½in).

YOU WILL NEED

1 piece of ecru 18-count Ainring, 29 × 28cm
   (11 × 11in)
DMC six-strand embroidery cotton
No. 26 tapestry needle
Masking tape
Square wooden tray

1. Complete the cross stitch, placing it centrally on the Ainring and using two strands of embroidery cotton throughout. Press the finished embroidery if required.

2. Place the embroidery face down on a clean, flat surface. Take the thick card provided with the tray and place it exactly in the centre of the embroidery. Fold the edges of the fabric over the card, working along one side and then along the opposite side, and securing the material in place with masking tape. When you are sure the design is centred, secure the corners firmly.

3. Insert the mounted embroidery into the tray, following the manufacturer's instructions.

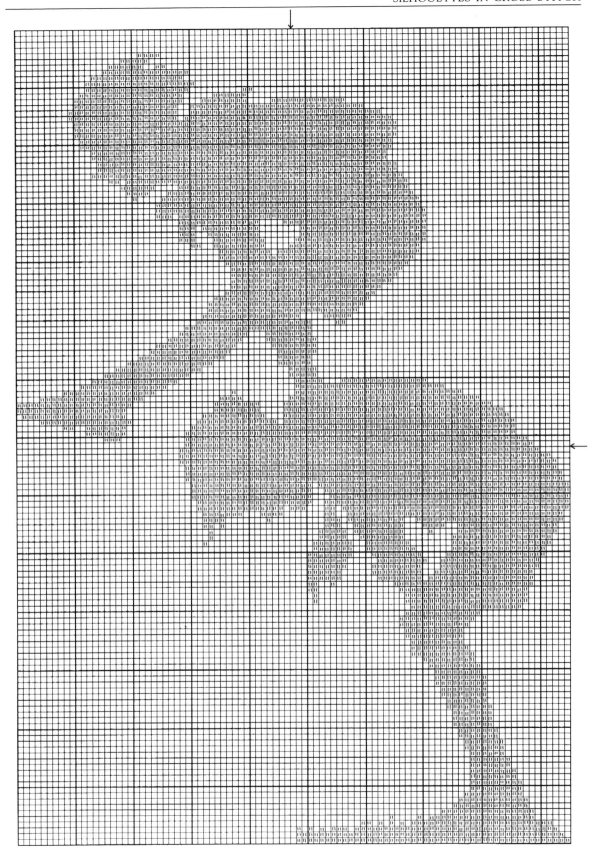

CARRIAGE CLOCK

CARRIAGE CLOCK

GRACE YOUR mantelpiece or dressing-table with this beautiful wooden carriage clock (see Suppliers, page 17). The materials given here are sufficient for a clock with the overall measurements of 16.5 × 13cm (6½ × 5in) with a face measuring 13 × 9cm (5 × 3½in).

YOU WILL NEED

1 piece of white 16-count Hardanger,
    20 × 16.5cm (8 × 6½in)
DMC six-strand embroidery cotton
No. 24 tapestry needle
Carriage clock
Strong thread for mounting embroidery

1. Complete the cross stitch, working it centrally on your piece of Hardanger and using two strands of cotton throughout. When you stitch the numerals, work one at a time and then finish off. Do not carry the thread from one to another, because it will show on the right side of the work. Locate the centre of your design. Mark a circle, 5mm (¼in) in diameter, on the embroidery and do not work that area. Stitch the design so that it will cover the mounting board enclosed with the clock. When the embroidery is complete, press it carefully to make sure that it is perfectly square and the weave of the fabric is straight.

2. Carefully unscrew the end cap, nut, washer and quartz movement from the clock. It may be necessary to remove the movement by turning it, as if you were unscrewing a nut. **Do not force the separation.** The clock hands will be packed separately in a plastic bag. Put all the parts in an envelope for later use.

3. Stretch the needlework around the mounting board, matching the centre holes. Fold the corners carefully, snipping away extra material so that you have a smooth, flat corner over the mounting board. Lace the vertical selvage edges together with needle and thread and check the position again to make sure the design is centred.

4. Use 5cm (2in) masking tape to secure the horizontal selvage edges to the back of the board. Make sure all is tight. With the needlework attached to the board, push a blunt object through the pre-marked centre. You will need to cut a small hole and enlarge it with a blunt object.

5. Assemble the carriage clock according to the manufacurer's instructions.

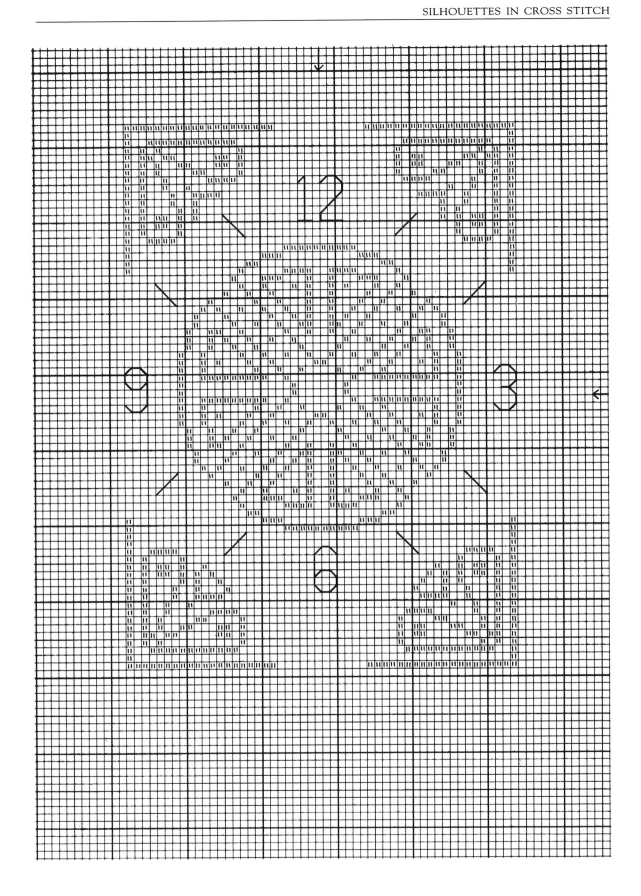

GEOMETRIC CUSHIONS

ALTHOUGH THESE designs are worked in cross stitch, they are based on Victorian blackwork designs. They are sure to make very striking accessories to enhance your bedroom or lounge. The materials quoted are sufficient to make one cushion measuring 25.5 × 25.5cm (10 × 10in), and the fabric measurements include a seam allowance of 12mm (½in).

YOU WILL NEED

1 piece of white 14-count Aida, 28 ×28cm
    (11 × 11cm)
1 piece of contrasting fabric of the same size, to
    back your cushion
2.4m (8ft) black lace, 4cm (1½in) deep, optional
1 25.5cm (10in) square cushion pad
DMC six-strand embroidery cotton
No. 24 tapestry needle
Sewing thread to match fabric

1. Complete the cross stitch embroidery, placing it centrally on the Aida and using two strands of cotton. When it is completed, press the work if necessary.
2. Lay the embroidery face up on a flat surface and pin the lace (if used) to the right side, making sure that the sewing edge of the lace lies just over the stitching line while the frill lies to the centre. Carefully tack the frill in to place, making sure that the lace is gathered evenly all the way around.
3. Place the backing material on the Aida, with right sides facing. Pin and tack three sides together making sure that you do not catch the lace in the seams.
4. Machine stitch around these three sides. Remove the pins and tacking stitches and turn to the right side.
5. Press in the seam allowance to the open edge, place the cushion pad inside the cover and oversew the open edge by hand.

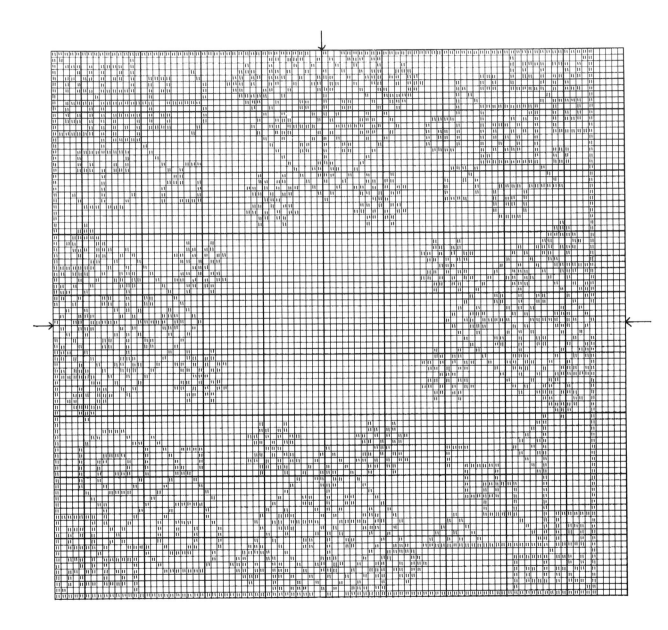

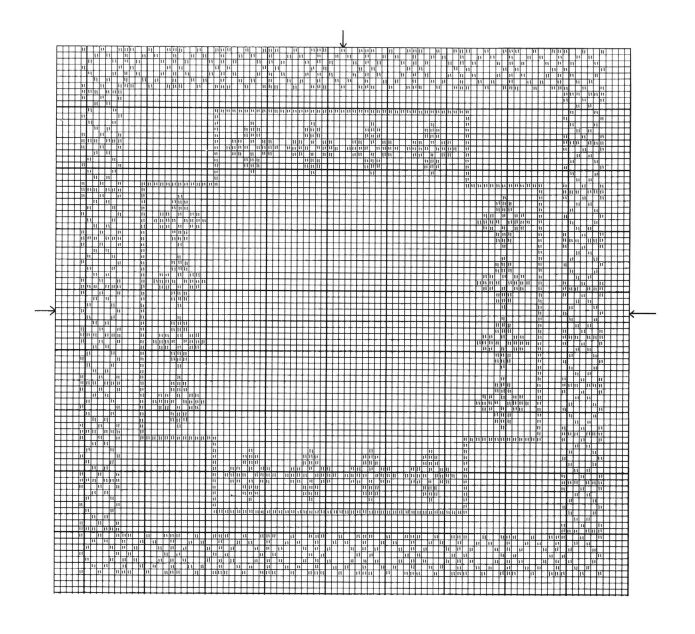

PLACE MATS

YOU CAN ADAPT the decorative borders on pages 60 and 61 to create striking place mats, which will brighten any dinner table. Alternatively you can make some highly individual and personal mats by stitching the silhouettes of your family. If you do not feel sufficiently confident about your artistic abilities to draw up a chart, take a profile photograph, making sure it is against a light background, and use a photocopier to enlarge or reduce it as necessary. Some office supply shops and stationers will photocopy onto graph paper for you; otherwise, make the pattern yourself. Remember to square up the edges of the shapes.

YOU WILL NEED
1 piece of 28-count linen 25 × 25cm (10 × 10in)
DMC six-strand embroidery cotton
No. 26 tapestry needle

1. Complete the cross stitch embroidery, placing it centrally on the linen. Use two strands of cotton and sew over two threads of the fabric, in effect making it 14-count. Press the completed work if necessary.
2. You will be left with approximately 4cm (1½in) of unworked linen all round the embroidery. To fray the edges of the place mats, simply remove one fabric thread at a time, until you have a frayed edge 1.5cm (½in) deep all round.

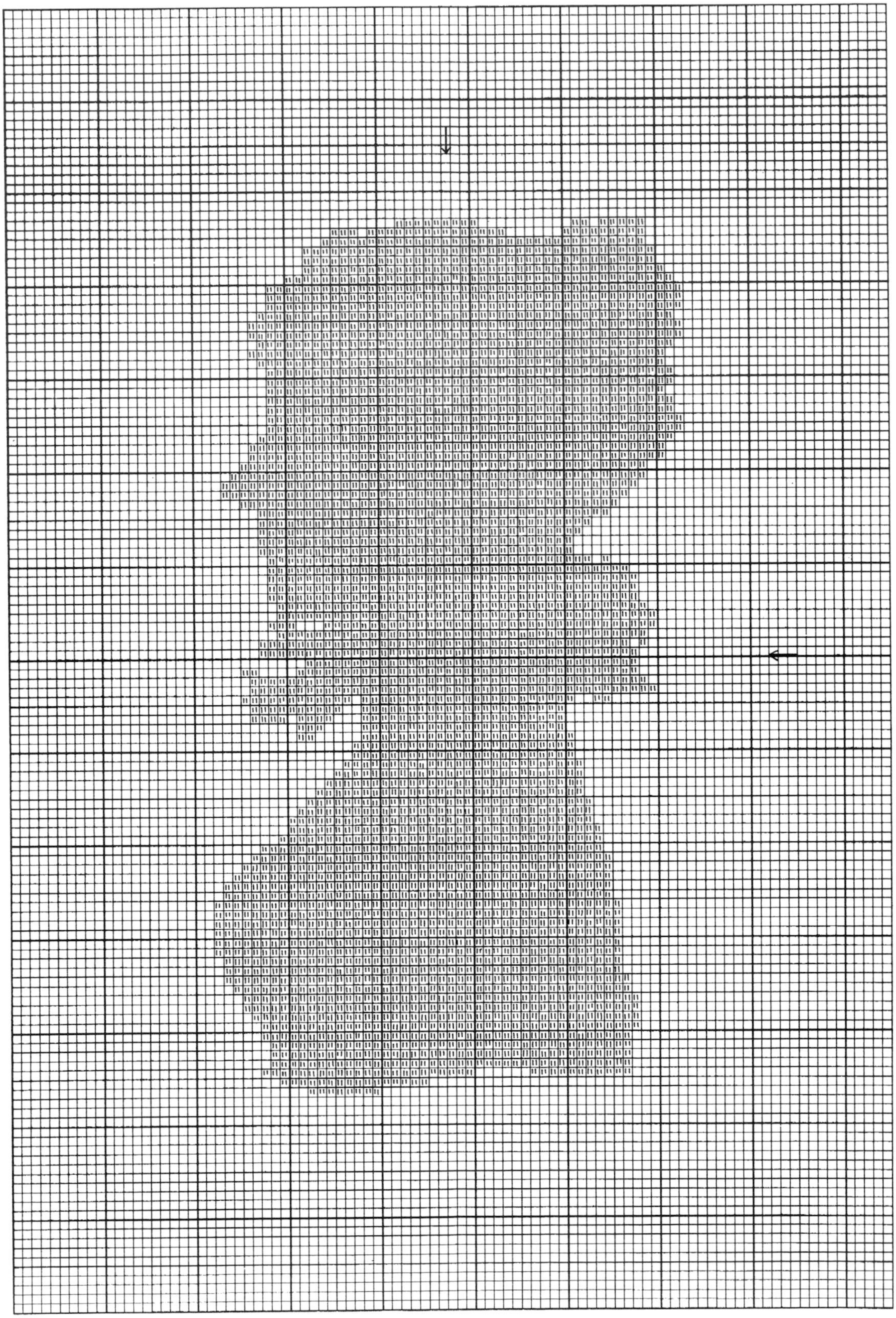

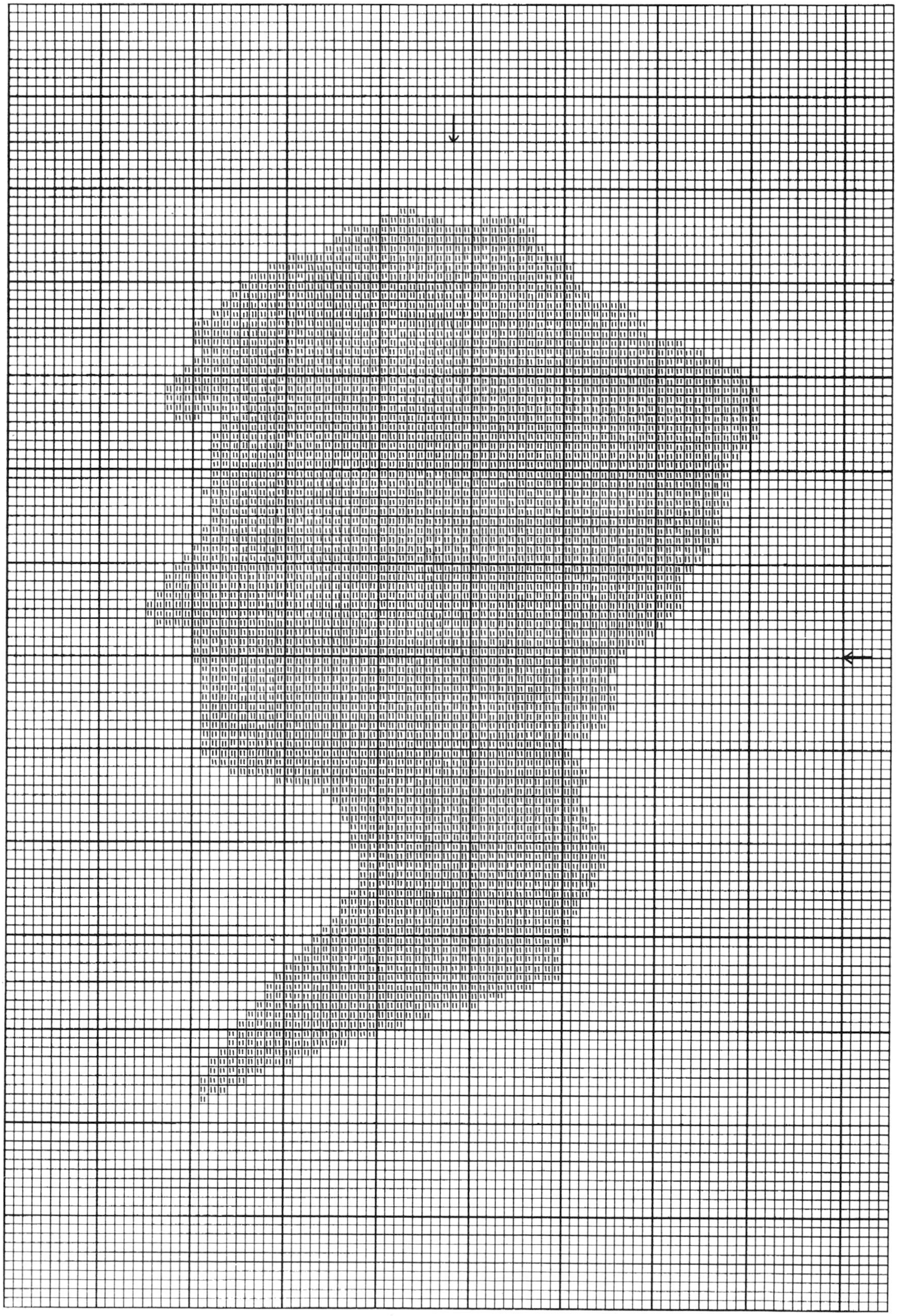

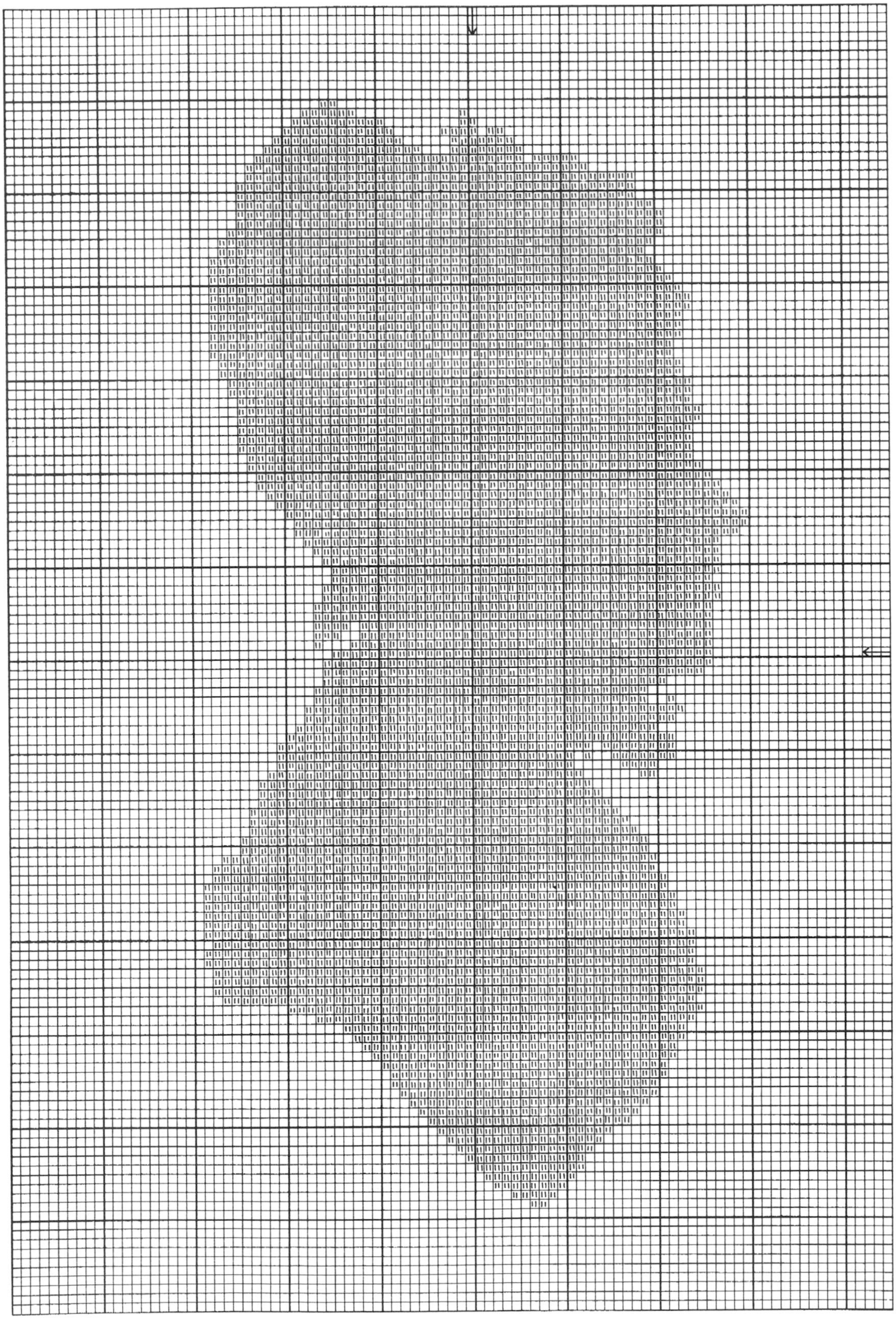

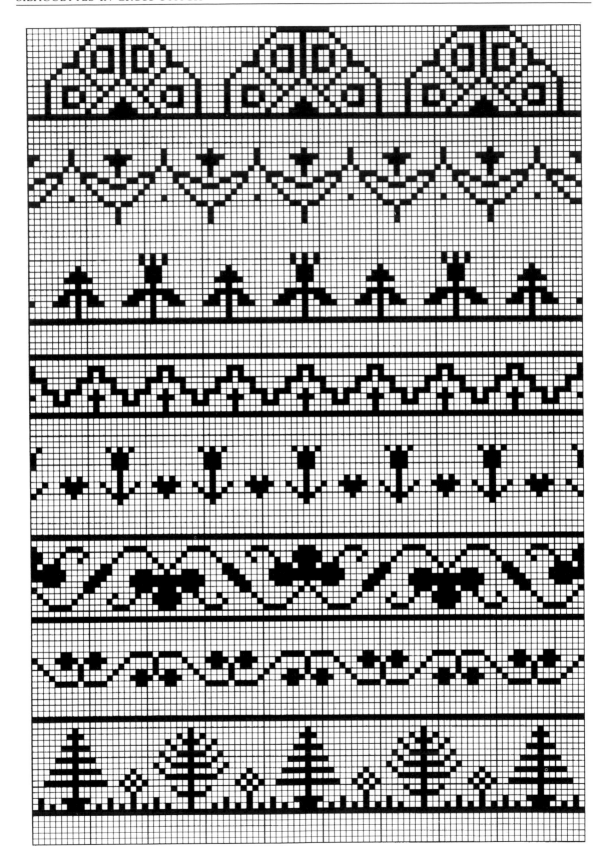

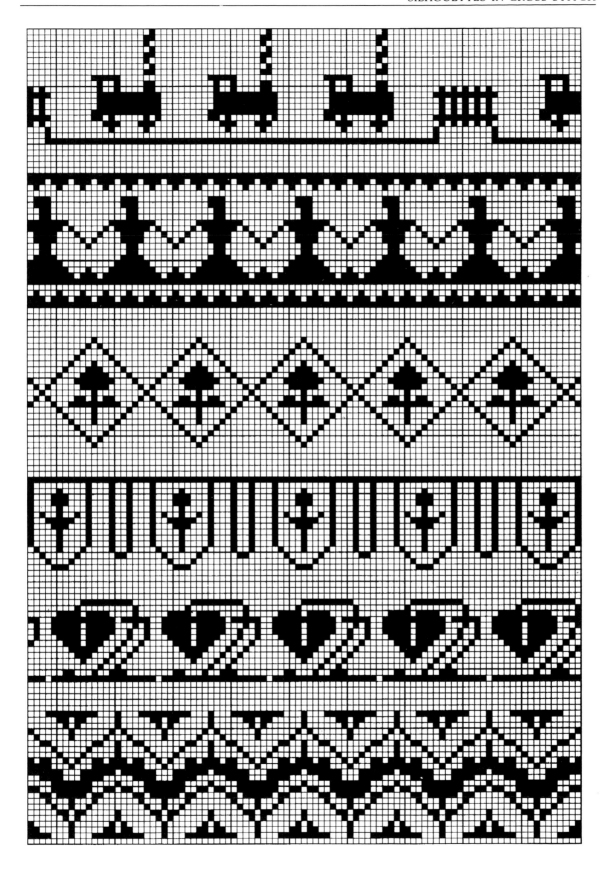

LACE-EDGED CUSHION

T HESE BEAUTIFUL lace-edged cushions are simple to make and will brighten up any room. They are pretty enough to go on a bed or on a favourite chair. The materials quoted here are sufficient to make one cushion measuring 30.5 × 30.5cm (12 × 12in), and the fabric measurements include a seam allowance of 12mm (½in).

YOU WILL NEED

1 piece of white 14-count Aida, 33 × 33cm
  (13 × 13in)
1 piece of contrasting fabric of the same size, to
  back your cushion
2.4m (8ft) black lace, 4cm (1½in) deep, gathered
1 30.5cm (12in) square cushion pad
DMC six-strand embroidery cotton
No. 24 tapestry needle
Sewing thread to match fabric

1. Complete the cross stitch embroidery, placing it centrally on the Aida. Work using three strands cotton throughout. When it is completed, press it if necessary.
2. Lay the embroidered material face up on a firm, flat surface and pin the lace to the right side, making sure that the sewing edge of the lace lies just over the stitching line while the frill lies to the centre. Tack it carefully so that the lace is gathered evenly all the way around. You will probably find it helpful to pin the lace to the Aida to keep it away from the seams.
3. Place the backing material on the Aida, with right sides facing. (The lace is sandwiched between the Aida and the backing fabric.) Pin and tack three sides together, making sure that you do not catch the lace in the seams.
4. Machine stitch around these three sides. Remove the pins and tacking stitches. Turn to the right side, so that the frill is released. Press in the seam allowance on the open edge. Place the cushion pad inside the cover and oversew the open edge by hand.

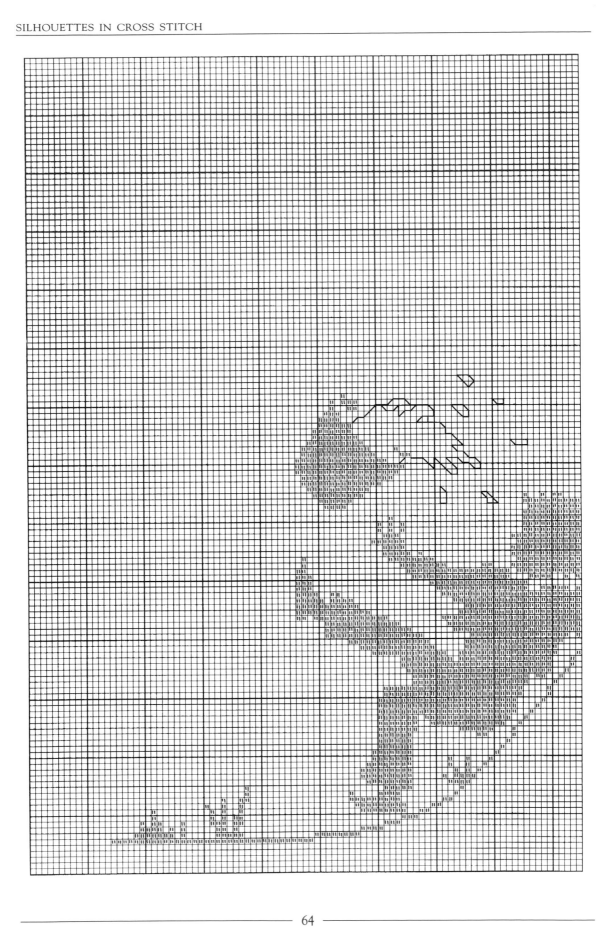

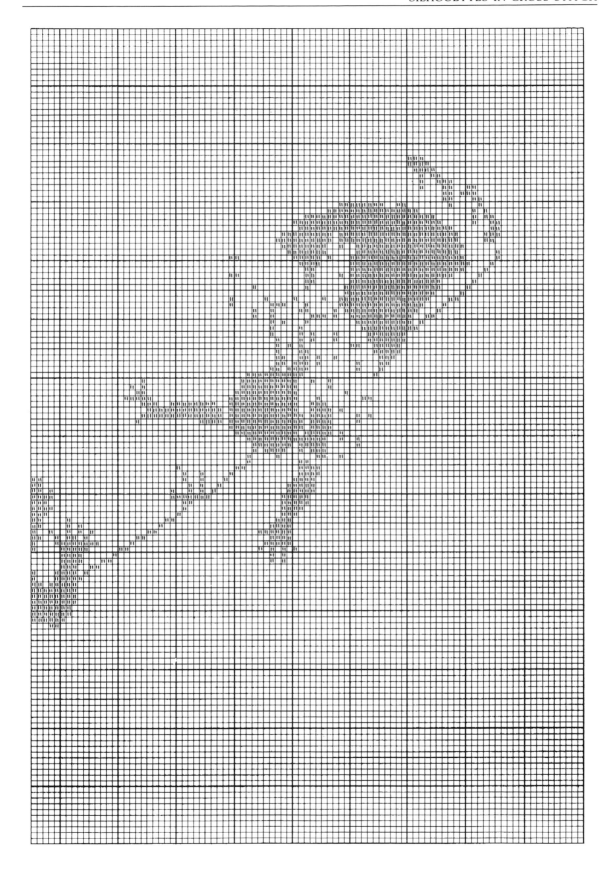

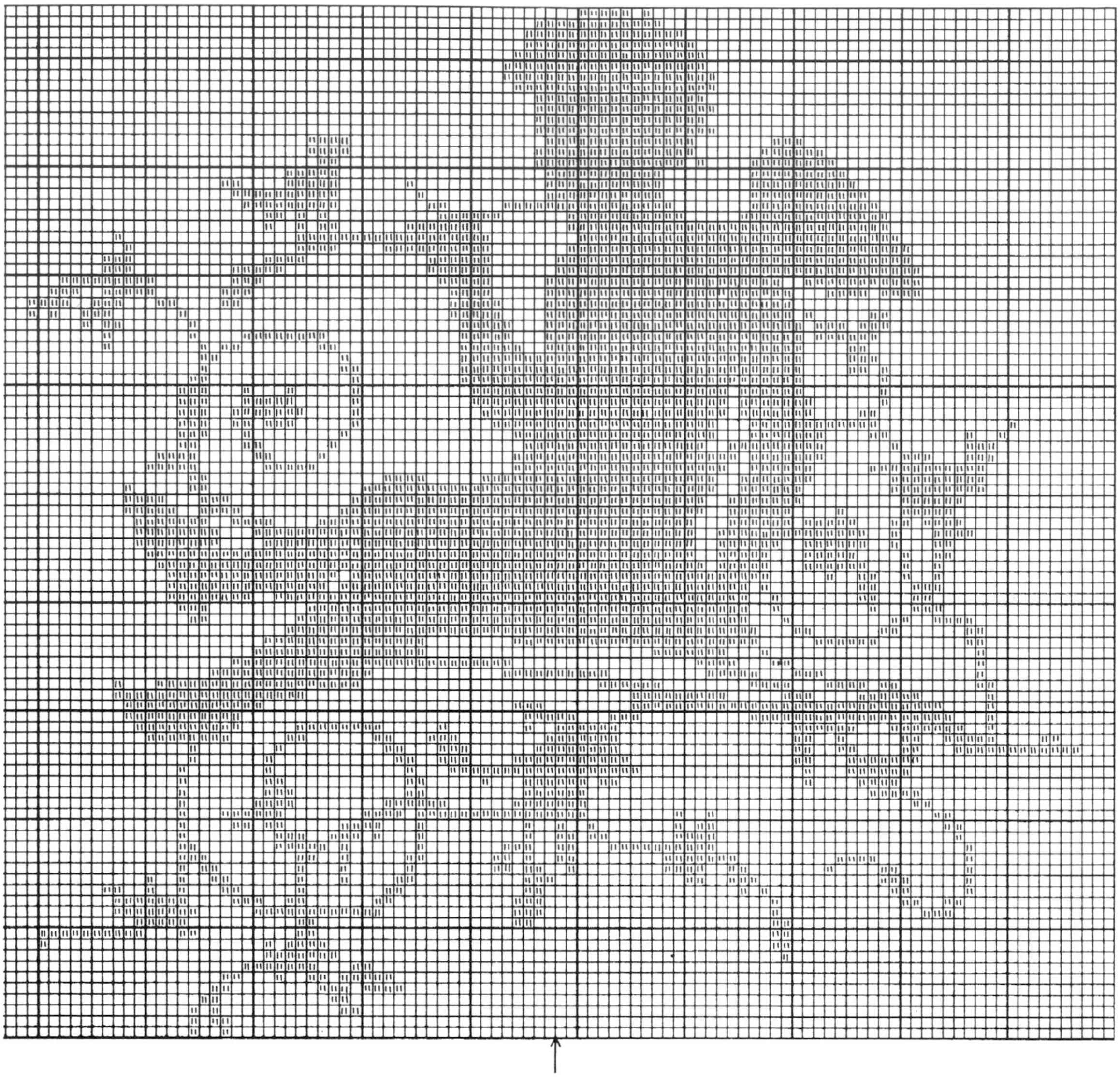

PORCELAIN TRINKET BOX

PORCELAIN TRINKET BOX

THESE BEAUTIFUL porcelain trinket boxes are both useful and decorative. They can be used to adorn a dressing-table, a small table or even a mantelpiece. A trinket box is an ideal present for any occasion or even just to say thank-you to someone special. The materials quoted here are sufficient for one trinket box with a lid 9cm (3½in) in diameter.

YOU WILL NEED

1 round porcelain trinket box with 9cm (3½in) diameter lid
1 piece of white 22-count Hardanger, 15 × 15cm (6 × 6in)
DMC six-strand embroidery cotton
No. 26 tapestry needle
All-purpose adhesive

1. Complete the cross stitch using one strand of cotton throughout. Press the completed work if necessary.
2. Place the finished embroidery face up on a firm, flat surface and carefully disassemble the parts of the trinket box lid. Use the rim of the lid to centralize the design, then draw around the outer edge on to the fabric. Remove the lid and cut the fabric to size. Oversew or stay stitch the raw edge if you wish or use a proprietary "fray check".
3. To assemble the lid, replace the clear acetate and place your design centrally into the lid, with the right side towards the acetate. Place the sponge behind your design. Push the metal locking disc firmly into place, using thumb pressure, with the raised side of the disc facing the sponge. When the locking disc is tightly in position, use a little all-purpose adhesive to secure the lid lining card to it.

GREETINGS CARD

A HAND-EMBROIDERED greetings card is a wonderful way of showing someone you care. Such a card will be treasured long after a shop-bought one has been forgotten. The materials quoted here are sufficient to make one card. If you make more than one at a time, you can sew several motifs on one piece of fabric, rather than cutting out several small pieces, as long as you space them well.

YOU WILL NEED

1 ready-made card with 7.5 × 11.5cm (3 × 4½in) rectangular cut-out
1 piece of 22-count Hardanger in the colour of your choice, 20 × 15cm (8 × 6in)
DMC six-strand embroidery cotton
No. 26 tapestry needle
Double-sided adhesive tape

1. Complete the cross stitch embroidery, using one strand of cotton.
2. When you have completed the embroidery, centralize the motif in the card "window" and trim the fabric to fit.
3. Use double-sided adhesive tape to fix the design into the card. Press the backing down firmly.

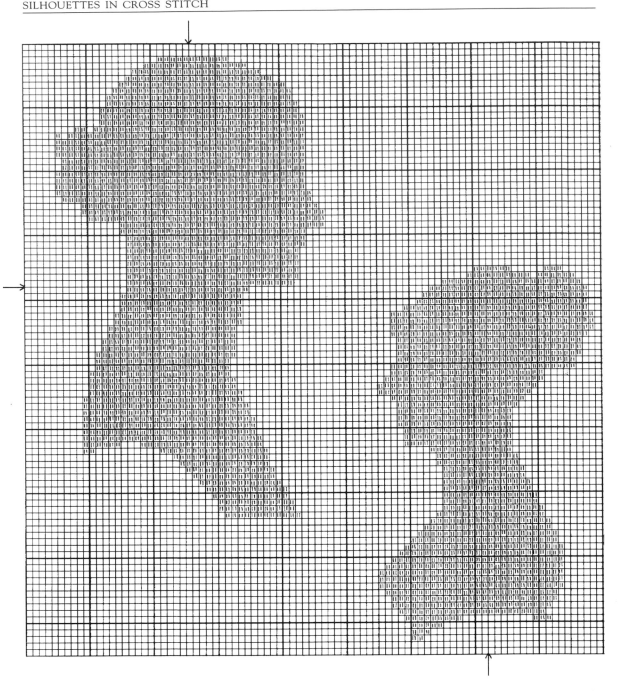

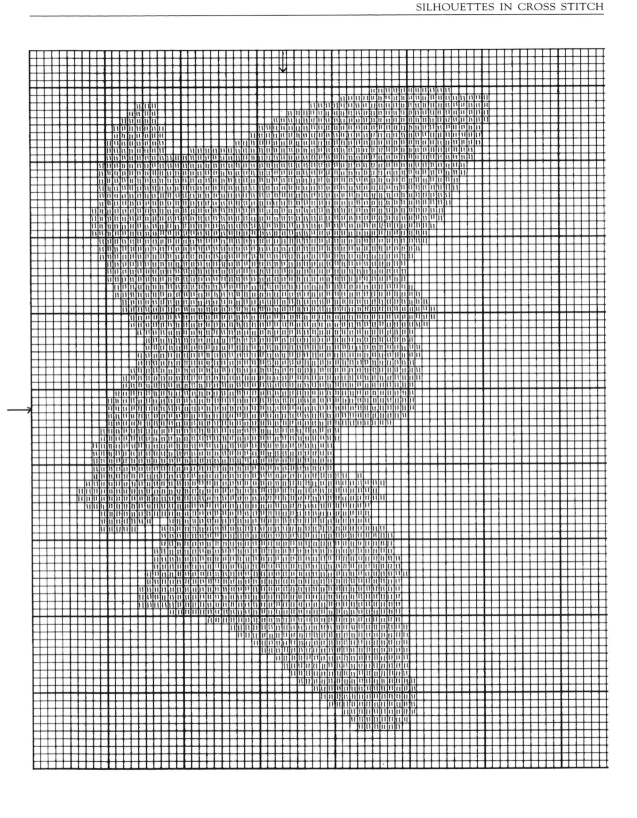

PAPERWEIGHT

P APERWEIGHTS make unusual gifts, which can be put to practical use on a desk or used as ornaments round the home.

YOU WILL NEED

Oval paperweight, 11.5 × 7.5cm (4½ × 3in)
1 piece of white 22-count Hardanger,
    18 × 12.5cm (7 × 5in)
DMC six-strand embroidery cotton
No. 26 tapestry needle

1. Complete the cross stitch, using one strand of cotton and making sure it is centrally placed on the fabric. Press the completed work if necessary.
2. Place the embroidery on a firm, flat surface and use the paper template (provided with the paperweight) to draw around your design, making sure that it is central. Cut the fabric to size and place it right side down into the recess on the base of the paperweight. Place the paper template on the reverse side of your embroidery. Peel the backing off the protective base and carefully stick it to the base of the paperweight, taking care that the embroidery and template do not move out of place.

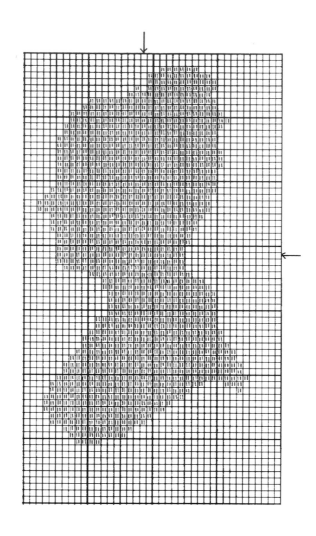